295

THE KAIROS DOCUMENT
Challenge to the Church

A Theological Comment on the Political Crisis in South Africa

Foreword by John W. de Gruchy

William B. Eerdmans Publishing Company
Grand Rapids, Michigan

First published 1985 by The Kairos Theologians, PO Box 32047, Braamfontein 2017, Republic of South Africa.

This edition first published 1986 by Wm. B. Eerdmans Publishing Co., 255 Jefferson Ave. SE, Grand Rapids, Mich. 49503

Printed in the United States of America

CONTENTS

Foreword

THE KAIROS DOCUMENT
A Radical Challenge to the Church in South Africa

Since the Cottesloe Consultation in 1960, many churches and theologians in South Africa have issued statements in opposition to apartheid. These have included pastoral letters, synodical resolutions, statements by particular groups and organizations, and confessional documents like the *Message to the People of South Africa* and the recent Belhar Confession of Faith issued by the Dutch Reformed Mission Church. The most recent, and undoubtedly the most radical, is the KAIROS document, first published at the end of September 1985.

Unlike the previous statements, the KAIROS document was not the work of some church-appointed commission. Although its origin was at the Institute for Contextual Theology in Johannesburg and although several well-known black theologians and the Dominican theologian Albert Nolan played an important role in the drafting and final editing of the document, it reflects the agonized thinking and reflecting of more than fifty black pastors working in the townships in and around Johannesburg. It is, in fact, the result of pastors and theologians sharing together in trying to develop theological perspectives for ministry in the midst of a national crisis. As the document itself claims, "this was a people's document." Originally, the participants had no intention of publishing it, but over the weeks, as it developed and was reworked in relation to the unfolding drama of social conflict, it took on increasing importance as a confessional statement addressed to the churches as well as the state.

In the Preface, the authors describe the document as "an attempt by concerned Christians in South Africa to reflect on the situation of death in our country. It is a critique of the current theological models that determine the type of activities the Church engages in to try to resolve the problems of the country. It is an attempt to develop, out of this perplexing situation, an alternative biblical and theological model that will in turn lead to forms of activity that will make a real difference to the future of our country." In developing its own "Prophetic Theology" over against what it calls "State Theology" and "Church Theology," the document identifies itself clearly with liberation theology's methodology and commitment.

Social analysis, the priority of praxis, and resistance to tyranny and oppression are fundamental themes. Equally fundamental is the document's rejection of the more liberal approaches which have hitherto characterized those churches which have opposed apartheid. In this respect it is particularly critical of the kind of statements which some church leaders have recently issued which have skirted the issues. Focusing on three stock ideas — reconciliation, justice, and nonviolence — the KAIROS document shows how these have been reduced to principles or cheapened because they have been neither understood in relation to social analysis nor allowed to become concrete political strategies which might lead to social transformation. Needless to say, the Document rejects even more categorically the recourse to a misuse of Romans 13 and "Law and Order" which characterize "State Theology" and lead to the idolatry of the state.

The final chapter of the document is a call to action. Once again in this respect it differs from other confessional statements because it not only issues the summons but also makes very specific suggestions, including acts of civil disobedience. Apart from the latter, perhaps the most controversial is its insistence that "the church must avoid becoming a 'Third Force,' a force between the oppressor and the oppressed." Rather, it maintains the church must identify itself fully with the movement for liberation and justice, even though this will sometimes require criticism.

The immediate response to the document was significant. One hundred fifty theologians, pastors, and laypersons, black and white, from around the country immediately signed it. Many more would have if they had been given the opportunity to do so, but speed was of the essence. Subsequently others have signed, and many who are basically committed to its thrust have offered a positive critique. This is important, for again, one of the differences between the KAIROS document and other statements is its provisional character. It does not claim to be complete or beyond criticism; on the contrary, it is intentionally open-ended, a basis for an on-going discussion arising out of action, analysis, and reflection. A second revised edition is already in preparation. By its very nature, quite apart from the dynamics of the South African situation, no theological statement of this kind could ever be final. Not, that is, if it is a witness to a living God at work in transforming history.

Professor of Christian Studies   JOHN W. DE GRUCHY
University of Cape Town

PREFACE

The KAIROS document is a Christian, biblical and theological comment on the political crisis in South Africa today. It is an attempt by concerned Christians in South Africa to reflect on the situation of death in our country. It is a critique of the current theological models that determine the type of activities the Church engages in to try to resolve the problems of the country. It is an attempt to develop, out of this perplexing situation, an alternative biblical and theological model that will in turn lead to forms of activity that will make a real difference to the future of our country.

Of particular interest is *the way* the theological material was produced. In June 1985 as the crisis was intensifying in the country, as more and more people were killed, maimed and imprisoned, as one black township after another revolted against the apartheid regime, as the people refused to be oppressed or to co-operate with oppressors, facing death by the day, and as the apartheid army moved into the townships to rule by the barrel of the gun, a number of theologians who were concerned about the situation expressed the need to reflect on this situation to determine what response by the Church and by all Christians in South Africa would be most appropriate.

A first discussion group met at the beginning of July in the heart of Soweto. Participants spoke freely about the situation and the various responses of the Church, Church leaders and Christians. A critique of these responses was made and the theology from which these responses flowed was also subjected to a critical analysis. Individual members of the group were assigned to put together material on specific themes which were raised during the discussion and to present the material to the next session of the group.

At the second meeting the material itself was subjected to a critique, and various people were commissioned to do more investigations on specific problematic areas. The latest findings, along with the rest of the material, were collated and presented to a third meeting of more than thirty people, consisting of theologians, ordinary Christians (lay theologians) and some Church leaders.

After a very extensive discussion some adjustments and additions were made, especially in regard to the section entitled 'Challenge to Action'. The group then appointed a committee to subject the document to further critique by various other Christian groupings throughout the country. Everybody was told that "this was a people's document which you can also own even by demolishing it if your position can stand the test of biblical faith and Christian experience in South Africa". They were told that this was an open-ended document which will never be said to be final.

The 'Working Committee', as it was called, was inundated with comments, suggestions and enthusiastic appreciation from various groups and individuals in the country. By the 13th September 1985 when the document was submitted for publication comments and recommendations were still flowing in. The first publication therefore must be taken as a beginning, a basis for further discussion by all Christians in the country. Further editions will be published later.

THE KAIROS DOCUMENT

Chapter One

THE MOMENT OF TRUTH

The time has come. The moment of truth has arrived. South Africa has been plunged into a crisis that is shaking the foundations and there is every indication that the crisis has only just begun and that it will deepen and become even more threatening in the months to come. It is the KAIROS or moment of truth not only for apartheid but also for the Church.

We as a group of theologians have been trying to understand the theological significance of this moment in our history. It is serious, very serious. For very many Christians in South Africa this is the KAIROS, the moment of grace and opportunity, the favourable time in which God issues a challenge to decisive action. It is a dangerous time because, if this opportunity is missed and allowed to pass by, the loss for the Church, for the Gospel and for all the people of South Africa will be immeasurable. Jesus wept over Jerusalem. He wept over the tragedy of the destruction of the city and the massacre of the people that was imminent, "and all because you did not recognise your opportunity (KAIROS) when God offered it" (Lk 19:44).

A crisis is a judgment that brings out the best in some people and the worst in others. A crisis is a moment of truth that shows us up for what we really are. There will be no place to hide and no way of pretending to be what we are not in fact. At this moment in South Africa the Church is about to be shown up for what it really is and no cover-up will be possible.

What the present crisis shows up, although many of us have known it all along, is that *the Church is divided*. More and more people are now saying that there are in fact two Churches in South Africa — a White Church and a Black Church. Even within the same denomination there are in fact two Churches. In the life and death conflict between different social forces that has come to a head in South Africa today, there are Christians (or at least people who profess to be Christians) on both sides of the conflict — and some who are trying to sit on the fence!

Does this prove that Christian faith has no real meaning or relevance for our times? Does it show that the Bible can be used for any purpose at all? Such problems would be critical enough for the Church in any circumstances, but when we also come to see that the conflict in South Africa is between the oppressor and the oppressed, the crisis for the Church as an institution becomes much more acute. Both oppressor and oppressed claim loyalty to the same Church. They are both baptised in the same baptism and participate together in the breaking of the same bread, the same body and blood of Christ. There we sit in the same Church while outside Christian policemen and soldiers are beating up and killing Christian children or torturing Christian prisoners to death while yet other Christians stand by and weakly plead for peace.

The Church is divided and its day of judgment has come.

The moment of truth has compelled us to analyse more carefully the different theologies in our Churches and to speak out more clearly and boldly about the real significance of these theologies. We have been able to isolate three theologies and we have chosen to call them 'State Theology', 'Church Theology' and 'Prophetic Theology'. In our thoroughgoing criticism of the first and second theologies we do not wish to mince our words. The situation is too critical for that.

Chapter Two

CRITIQUE OF
STATE THEOLOGY

The South African apartheid State has a theology of its own and we have chosen to call it 'State Theology'. 'State Theology' is simply the theological justification of the status quo with its racism, capitalism and totalitarianism. It blesses injustice, canonises the will of the powerful and reduces the poor to passivity, obedience and apathy.

How does 'State Theology' do this? It does it by misusing theological concepts and biblical texts for its own political purposes. In this document we would like to draw your attention to four key examples of how this is done in South Africa. The first would be the use of Romans 13:1-7 to give an absolute and 'divine' authority to the State. The second would be the use of the idea of 'Law and Order' to determine and control what the people may be permitted to regard as just and unjust. The third would be the use of the word 'communist' to brand anyone who rejects 'State Theology'. And finally there is the use that is made of the name of God.

2.1 Romans 13:1-7
The misuse of this famous text is not confined to the present government in South Africa. Throughout the history of Christianity totalitarian regimes have tried to legitimise an attitude of blind obedience and absolute servility towards the state by quoting this text. The well-known theologian Oscar Cullmann pointed this out thirty years ago:

> As soon as Christians, out of loyalty to the gospel of Jesus, offer resistance to a State's totalitarian claim, the representatives of the State or their collaborationist theological advisers are accustomed to appeal

to this saying of Paul, as if Christians are here com-
mended to endorse and thus to abet all the crimes
of a totalitarian State.
(*The State in the New Testament* [1957], p 56.)

But what then is the meaning of Romans 13:1-7 and
why is the use made of it by 'State Theology' unjustifiable from a biblical point of view?

'State Theology' assumes that in this text Paul is
presenting us with the absolute and definitive Christian doctrine about the State, in other words an absolute and universal principle that is equally valid for
all times and in all circumstances. The falseness of this
assumption has been pointed out by numerous biblical
scholars (see, for example, E Kasemann, *Commentary
on Romans* [1980]; O Cullmann, *The State in the New
Testament* [1957]).

What has been overlooked here is one of the most
fundamental of all principles of biblical interpretation:
every text must be interpreted *in its context*. To abstract
a text from its context and to interpret it in the abstract
is to distort the meaning of God's Word. Moreover, the
context here is not only the chapters and verses that
precede and succeed this particular text nor is it even
limited to the total context of the Bible. The context
includes also the *circumstances* in which Paul's statement was made. Paul was writing to a particular Christian community in Rome, a community that had its
own particular problems in relation to the State at that
time and in those circumstances. That is part of the
context of our text.

Many authors have drawn attention to the fact that
in the rest of the Bible God does not demand obedience
to oppressive rulers. Examples can be given ranging
from Pharaoh to Pilate and through into Apostolic

times. The Jews and later the Christians did not believe that their imperial overlords, the Egyptians, the Babylonians, the Greeks or the Romans, had some kind of divine right to rule them and oppress them. These empires were the beasts described in the Book of Daniel and the Book of Revelation. God *allowed* them to rule for a while but he did not *approve* of what they did. It was not God's will. His will was the freedom and liberation of Israel. Romans 13:1-7 cannot be contradicting all of this.

But most revealing of all is the circumstances of the Roman Christians to whom Paul was writing. They were not revolutionaries. They were not trying to overthrow the State. They were not calling for a change of government. They were what has been called, 'antinomians' or 'enthusiasts' and their belief was that Christians, and only Christians, were exonerated from obeying any State at all, any government or political authority at all, *because* Jesus alone was their Lord and King. This is of course heretical, and Paul is compelled to point out to these Christians that before the second coming of Christ there will always be some kind of State, some kind of secular government and that Christians are not exonerated from subjection to some kind of political authority.

Paul is simply not addressing the issue of a just or unjust State or the need to change one government for another. He is simply establishing the fact that there will be some kind of secular authority and that Christians as such are not exonerated from subjection to secular laws and authorities. He does not say anything at all about what they should do when the State becomes unjust and oppressive. That is another question.

Consequently those who try to find answers to the

very different questions and problems of our time in the text of Romans 13:1-7 are doing a great disservice to Paul. The use that 'State Theology' makes of this text tells us more about the political options of those who construct this theology than it does about the meaning of God's Word in this text. As one biblical scholar puts it: "The primary concern is to justify the interests of the State, and the text is pressed into its service without respect for the context and the intention of Paul".

If we wish to search the Bible for guidance in a situation where the State that is supposed to be "the servant of God" (Romans 13:16) betrays that calling and begins to serve Satan instead, then we can study chapter 13 of the Book of Revelation. Here the Roman State becomes the servant of the dragon (the devil) and takes on the appearance of a horrible beast. Its days are numbered because God will not permit his unfaithful servant to reign forever.

2.2 Law and Order

The State makes use of the concept of law and order to maintain the status quo which it depicts as 'normal'. But this *law* is the unjust and discriminatory laws of apartheid and this *order* is the organised and institutionalised disorder of oppression. Anyone who wishes to change this law and this order is made to feel that they are lawless and disorderly. In other words they are made to feel guilty of sin.

It is indeed the duty of the State to maintain law and order, but it has not divine mandate to maintain any kind of law and order. Something does not become moral and just simply because the State has declared it to be a law and the organisation of a society is not a just and right order simply because it has been instituted by the State. We cannot accept any kind of law and any kind of order. The concern of Christians is that we should have in our country a just law and a right order.

In the present crisis and especially during the State of Emergency, 'State Theology' has tried to re-establish the status quo of orderly discrimination, exploitation and oppression by appealing to the consciences of its citizens in the name of law and order. It tries to make those who reject this law and this order feel that they are ungodly. The State here is not only usurping the right of the Church to make judgments about what would be right and just in our circumstances; it is going even further than that and demanding of us, in the name of law and order, an obedience that must be reserved for God alone. The South African State recognises no authority beyond itself and therefore it will not allow anyone to question what it has chosen to define as 'law and order'. However, there are millions of Christians in South Africa today who are saying with Peter: "We must obey God rather than man (human beings)" (Acts 5:29).

2.3 The Threat of Communism

We all know how the South African State makes use of the label 'communist'. Anything that threatens the status quo is labelled 'communist'. Anyone who opposes the State and especially anyone who rejects its theology is simply dismissed as a 'communist'. No account is taken of what communism really means. No thought is given to why some people have indeed opted for communism or for some form of socialism. Even people who have not rejected capitalism are called 'communists' when they reject 'State Theology'. The State uses the label 'communist' in an uncritical and unexamined way as its symbol of evil.

'State Theology' like every other theology needs to have its own concrete symbol of evil. It must be able to symbolise what it regards as godless behaviour and what ideas must be regarded as atheistic. It must have its own version of hell. And so it has invented, or rather taken over, the myth of communism. All evil is communistic and all communist or socialist ideas are atheistic and godless. Threats about hell-fire and eternal damnation are replaced by threats and warnings about the horrors of a tyrannical, totalitarian, atheistic and terrorist communist regime — a kind of hell-on-earth. This is a very convenient way of frightening some people into accepting any kind of domination and exploitation by a capitalist minority.

The South African State has its own heretical theology, and according to that theology millions of Christians in South Africa (not to mention the rest of the world) are to be regarded as 'atheists'. It is significant that in earlier times when Christians rejected the gods of the Roman Empire they were branded as 'atheists' — by the State.

2.4 The God of the State

The State in its oppression of the people makes use again and again of the name of God. Military chaplains use it to encourage the South African Defence Force, police chaplains use it to strengthen policemen and cabinet ministers use it in their propaganda speeches. But perhaps the most revealing of all is the blasphemous use of God's holy name in the preamble to the new apartheid constitution.

> In humble submission to Almighty God, who controls the destinies of nations and the history of peoples; who gathered our forebears together from many lands and gave them this their own; who has guided them from generation to generation; who has wondrously delivered them from the dangers that beset them.

This god is an idol. It is as mischievous, sinister and evil as any of the idols that the prophets of Israel had to contend with. Here we have a god who is historically on the side of the white settlers, who dispossesses black people of their land and who gives the major part of the land to his "chosen people".

It is the god of superior weapons who conquered those who were armed with nothing but spears. It is the god of the casspirs and hippos, the god of teargas, rubber bullets, sjamboks, prison cells and death sentences. Here is a god who exalts the proud and humbles the poor—the very opposite of the God of the Bible who "scatters the proud of heart, pulls down the mighty from their thrones and exalts the humble" (Lk 1:51-52). From a theological point of view the opposite of the God of the Bible is the devil, Satan. The god of the South African State is not merely an idol or false god, it is the devil disguised as Almighty God—the antichrist.

The oppressive South African regime will always be particularly abhorrent to Christians precisely because it makes use of Christianity to justify its evil ways. As Christians we simply cannot tolerate this blasphemous use of God's name and God's Word. 'State Theology' is not only heretical, it is blasphemous. Christians who are trying to remain faithful to the God of the Bible are even more horrified when they see that there are Churches, like the White Dutch Reformed Churches and other groups of Christians, who actually subscribe to this heretical theology. 'State Theology' needs its own prophets and it manages to find them from the ranks of those who profess to be ministers of God's Word in some of our Churches. What is particularly tragic for a Christian is to see the number of people who are fooled and confused by these false prophets and their heretical theology.

Chapter Three

CRITIQUE OF
'CHURCH THEOLOGY'

We have analysed the statements that are made from time to time by the so-called 'English-speaking' Churches. We have looked at what Church leaders tend to say in their speeches and press statements about the apartheid regime and the present crisis. What we found running through all these pronouncements is a series of inter-related theological assumptions. These we have chosen to call 'Church Theology'. We are well aware of the fact that this theology does *not* express the faith of the majority of Christians in South Africa today who form the greater part of most of our Churches. Nevertheless the opinions expressed by Church leaders are regarded in the media and generally in our society as the official opinions of the Churches. We have therefore chosen to call these opinions 'Church Theology'. The crisis in which we find ourselves today compels us to question this theology, to question its assumptions, its implications and its practicality.

In a limited, guarded and cautious way this theology is critical of apartheid. Its criticism, however, is superficial and counter-productive because instead of engaging in an in-depth analysis of the signs of our times, it relies upon a few stock ideas derived from Christian tradition and then uncritically and repeatedly applies them to our situation. The stock ideas used by almost all these Church leaders that we would like to examine here are: reconciliation (or peace), justice and non-violence.

3.1 Reconciliation
'Church Theology' takes 'reconciliation' as the key to problem resolution. It talks about the need for recon-

ciliation between white and black, or between all South Africans. 'Church Theology' often describes the Christian stance in the following way: "We must be fair. We must listen to both sides of the story. If the two sides can only meet to talk and negotiate they will sort out their differences and misunderstandings, and the conflict will be resolved". On the face of it this may sound very Christian. But is it?

The fallacy here is that 'reconciliation' has been made into an absolute principle that must be applied in all cases of conflict or dissension. But not all cases of conflict are the same. We can imagine a private quarrel between two people or two groups whose differences are based upon misunderstandings. In such cases it would be appropriate to talk and negotiate to sort out the misunderstandings and to reconcile the two sides. But there are other conflicts in which one side is right and the other wrong. There are conflicts where one side is a fully armed and violent oppressor while the other side is defenceless and oppressed. There are conflicts that can only be described as the struggle between justice and injustice, good and evil, God and the devil. To speak of reconciling these two is not only a mistaken application of the Christian idea of reconciliation, it is a total betrayal of all that Christian faith has ever meant. Nowhere in the Bible or in Christian tradition has it ever been suggested that we ought to try to reconcile good and evil, God and the devil. We are supposed to do away with evil, injustice, oppression and sin — not come to terms with it. We are supposed to oppose, confront and reject the devil and not try to sup with the devil.

In our situation in South Africa today it would be totally unChristian to plead for reconciliation and peace before the present injustices have been removed. Any such plea plays into the hands of the oppressor by trying to persuade those of us who are oppressed to accept our oppression and to become reconciled to the intolerable crimes that are committed against us. That is not Christian reconciliation, it is sin. It is asking us to become accomplices in our own oppression, to become servants of the devil. No reconciliation is possible in South Africa *without justice*.

What this means in practice is that no reconciliation, no forgiveness and no negotiations are possible *without repentance*. The Biblical teaching on reconciliation and forgiveness makes it quite clear that nobody can be forgiven and reconciled with God unless he or she repents of their sins. Nor are *we* expected to forgive the unrepentant sinner. When he or she repents we must be willing to forgive seventy times seven times, but before that, we are expected to preach repentance to those who sin against us or against anyone. Reconciliation, forgiveness and negotiations will become our Christian duty in South Africa only when the apartheid regime shows signs of genuine repentance. The recent speech of P W Botha in Durban, the continued military repression of the people in the townships and the jailing of all its opponents is clear proof of the total lack of repentance on the part of the present regime.

There is nothing that we want more than true reconciliation and genuine peace — the peace that God wants and not the peace the world wants (Jn 14:27). The peace that God wants is based upon truth, repentance, justice and love. The peace that the world offers us is a unity that compromises the truth, covers over injustice and oppression and is totally motivated by selfishness. At this stage, like Jesus, we must expose this false peace, confront our oppressors and sow dissension. As Christians we must say with Jesus: "Do you suppose that I am here to bring peace on earth. No, I tell you, but rather dissension" (Lk 12:51). There can be no real peace without justice and it would be quite wrong to try to preserve 'peace' and 'unity' at all costs, even at the cost of truth and justice and, worse still, at the cost of thousands of young lives. As disciples of Jesus we should rather promote truth and justice and life at all costs, even at the cost of creating conflict, disunity and dissension along the way. To be truly biblical our Church leaders must adopt a theology that millions of Christians have already adopted — a biblical theology of direct confrontation with the forces of evil rather than a theology of reconciliation with sin and the devil.

3.2 Justice

It would be quite wrong to give the impression that Church Theology' in South Africa is not particularly concerned about the need for justice. There have been some very strong and very sincere demands for justice. But the question we need to ask here, the very serious theological question is: What kind of justice? An examination of Church statements and pronouncements gives the distinct impression that the justice that is envisaged is *the justice of reform,* that is to say, a justice that is determined by the oppressor, by the white minority and that is offered to the people as a kind of concession. It does not appear to be the more radical justice that comes from below and is determined by the people of South Africa.

One of our main reasons for drawing this conclu-

sion is the simple fact that almost all Church statements and appeals are made to the State or to the
white community. The assumption seems to be that
changes must come from whites or at least from people
who are at the top of the pile. The general idea appears
to be that one must simply appeal to the conscience
and the goodwill of those who are responsible for injustice in our land and that once they have repented
of their sins and after some consultation with others
they will introduce the necessary reforms to the system. Why else would Church leaders be having talks
with P W Botha if this is not the vision of a just and
peaceful solution to our problems?

At the heart of this approach is the reliance upon
'individual conversions' in response to 'moralising demands' to change the structures of a society. It has not
worked and it never will work. The present crisis with
all its cruelty, brutality and callousness is ample proof
of the ineffectiveness of years and years of Christian
'moralising' about the need for love. The problem that
we are dealing with here in South Africa is not merely
a problem of personal guilt, it is a problem of structural
injustice. People are suffering, people are being maimed
and killed and tortured every day. We cannot just sit
back and wait for the oppressor to see the light so that
the oppressed can put out their hands and beg for the
crumbs of some small reforms. That in itself would be
degrading and oppressive.

There have been reforms and, no doubt, there will
be further reforms in the near future. And it may well
be that the Church's appeal to the consciences of whites
has contributed marginally to the introduction of some
of these reforms. But can such reforms ever be regarded as real change, as the introduction of a true and

lasting justice. Reforms that come from the top are never satisfactory. They seldom do more than make the oppression more effective and more acceptable. If the oppressor does ever introduce reforms that might lead to real change this will come about because of strong pressure from those who are oppressed. True justice, God's justice, demands a radical change of structures. This can only come from below, from the oppressed themselves. God will bring about change through the oppressed as he did through the oppressed Hebrew slaves in Egypt. God does not bring his justice through reforms introduced by the Pharaohs of this world.

Why then does 'Church Theology' appeal to the top rather than to the people who are suffering? Why does this theology not demand that the oppressed stand up for their rights and wage a struggle against their oppressors? Why does it not tell them that it is *their* duty to work for justice and to change the unjust structures? Perhaps the answer to these questions is that appeals from the 'top' in the Church tend very easily to be appeals to the 'top' in society. An appeal to the conscience of those who perpetuate the system of injustice must be made. But real change and true justice can only come from below, from the people—most of whom are Christians.

3.3 Non-violence
The stance of 'Church Theology' on non-violence, expressed as a blanket condemnation of all that is *called* violence, has not only been unable to curb the violence of our situation, it has actually, although unwittingly, been a major contributing factor in the recent

escalation of State violence. Here again non-violence has been made into an absolute principle that applies to anything anyone *calls* violence without regard for who is using it, which side they are on or what purpose they may have in mind. In our situation, this is simply counter-productive.

The problem for the Church here is the way the word violence is being used in the propaganda of the State. The State and the media have chosen to call violence what some people do in the townships as they struggle for their liberation, i.e. throwing stones, burning cars and buildings and sometimes killing collaborators. But this *excludes* the structural, institutional and unrepentant violence of the State and especially the oppressive and naked violence of the police and the army. These things are not counted as violence. And even when they are acknowledged to be 'excessive', they are called 'misconduct' or even 'atrocities' but never violence. Thus the phrase 'violence in the townships' comes to mean what the young people are doing and not what the police are doing or what apartheid in general is doing to people. If one calls for non-violence in such circumstances one appears to be criticising the resistance of the people while justifying or at least overlooking the violence of the police and the State. That is how it is understood not only by the State and its supporters but also by the people who are struggling for their freedom. Violence, especially in our circumstances, is a loaded word.

It is true that Church statements and pronouncements do also condemn the violence of the police. They do say that they condemn *all violence*. But is it legitimate, especially in our circumstances, to use the same word violence in a blanket condemnation to cover the ruthless and repressive activities of the State and the desperate attempts of the people to defend themselves? Do such abstractions and generalisations not confuse the issue? How can acts of oppression, injustice and domination be equated with acts of resistance and self-defence? Would it be legitimate to describe both the physical force used by a rapist and the physical force used by a woman trying to resist the rapist as violence?

Moreover, there is nothing in the Bible or in our Christian tradition that would permit us to make such generalisations. Throughout the Bible the word violence is used to describe everything that is done by a wicked oppressor (e.g. Ps 72:12-14; Is 59:1-8; Jer 22:13-17; Amos 3:9-10; 6:3; Mic 2:2; 3:1-3; 6:12). It is never used to describe the activities of Israel's armies in attempting to liberate themselves or to resist aggression. When Jesus says that we should turn the other cheek he is telling us that we must not take revenge; he is not saying that we should never defend ourselves or others. There is a long and consistent Christian tradition about the use of physical force to defend oneself against aggressors and tyrants. In other words there are circumstances when physical force may be used. They are very restrictive circumstances, only as the very last resort and only as the lesser of two evils, or, as Bonhoeffer put it, "the lesser of two guilts". But it is simply not true to say that every possible use of physical force is violence and that no matter what the circumstances may be it is never permissible.

This is not to say that any use of force at any time by people who are oppressed is permissible simply because they are struggling for their liberation. There have been cases of killing and maiming that no Christian would want to approve of. But then our disapproval is based upon a concern for genuine liberation and a conviction that such acts are unnecessary, counter-productive and unjustifiable and not because they fall under a blanket condemnation of any use of physical force in any circumstances.

And finally what makes the professed non-violence of 'Church Theology' extremely suspect in the eyes of very many people, including ourselves, is the tacit support that many Church leaders give to the growing *militarisation* of the South African State. How can one condemn all violence and then appoint chaplains to a very violent and oppressive army? How can one condemn all violence and then allow young white males to accept their conscription into the armed forces? Is it because the activities of the armed forces and the police are counted as defensive? That raises very serious questions about whose side such Church leaders might be on. Why are the activities of young blacks in the townships not regarded as defensive?

In practice what one calls 'violence' and what one calls 'self-defence' seems to depend upon which side one is on. To call all physical force 'violence' is to try to be neutral and to refuse to make a judgment about who is right and who is wrong. The attempt to remain neutral in this kind of conflict is futile. Neutrality enables the status quo of oppression (and therefore violence) to continue. It is a way of giving tacit support to the oppressor.

3.4 The Fundamental Problem

It is not enough to criticise 'Church Theology'; we must also try to account for it. What is behind the mistakes and misunderstandings and inadequacies of this theology?

In the first place we can point to a lack of *social analysis*. We have seen how 'Church Theology' tends to make use of absolute principles like reconciliation, negotiation, non-violence and peaceful solutions and applies them indiscriminately and uncritically to all situations. Very little attempt is made to analyse what is actually happening in our society and why it is happening. It is not possible to make valid moral judgments about a society without first understanding that society. The analysis of apartheid that underpins 'Church Theology' is simply inadequate. The present crisis has now made it very clear that the efforts of Church leaders to promote effective and practical ways of changing our society have failed. This failure is due in no small measure to the fact that 'Church Theology' has not developed a social analysis that would enable it to understand the mechanics of injustice and oppression.

Closely linked to this is the lack in 'Church Theology' of an adequate understanding of *politics and political strategy*. Changing the structures of a society is fundamentally a matter of politics. It requires a political strategy based upon a clear social or political analysis. The Church has to address itself to these strategies and to the analysis upon which they are based. It is into this political situation that the Church has to bring the gospel. Not as an alternative solution to our problems as if the gospel provided us with a non-political solution to political problems. There is no specifically Christian solution. There will be a Christian way of approaching the political solutions, a Christian spirit and motivation and attitude. But there is no way of bypassing politics and political strategies.

But we have still not pinpointed the fundamental problem. Why has 'Church Theology' not developed a social analysis? Why does it have an inadequate understanding of the need for political strategies? And why does it make a virtue of neutrality and sitting on the sidelines?

The answer must be sought in the *type of faith and spirituality* that has dominated Church life for centuries. As we all know, spirituality has tended to be an other-worldly affair that has very little, if anything at all, to do with the affairs of this world. Social and political matters were seen as worldly affairs that have nothing to do with the spiritual concerns of the Church. Moreover, spirituality has also been understood to be purely private and individualistic. Public affairs and social problems were thought to be beyond the sphere of spirituality. And finally the spirituality we inherit tends to rely upon God to intervene in his own good time to put right what is wrong in the world. That leaves very little for human beings to do except to pray for God's intervention.

It is precisely this kind of spirituality that, when faced with the present crisis in South Africa, leaves so many Christians and Church leaders in a state of near paralysis.

It hardly needs saying that this kind of faith and this type of spirituality has no biblical foundation. The Bible does not separate the human person from the world in which he or she lives; it does not separate the individual from the social or one's private life from one's public life. God redeems the whole person as part of his whole creation (Rom 8:18-24). A truly biblical spirituality would penetrate into every aspect of human existence and would exclude nothing from God's redemptive will. Biblical faith is prophetically relevant to everything that happens in the world.

Chapter Four

TOWARDS A
PROPHETIC THEOLOGY

Our present KAIROS calls for a response from Christians that is biblical, spiritual, pastoral and, above all, prophetic. It is not enough in these circumstances to repeat generalised Christian principles. We need a bold and incisive response that is prophetic because it speaks to the particular circumstances of this crisis, a response that does not give the impression of sitting on the fence but is clearly and unambiguously taking a stand.

4.1 Social Analysis

The first task of a prophetic theology for our times would be an attempt at social analysis or what Jesus would call "reading the signs of the times" (Mt 16:3) or "interpreting this KAIROS" (Lk 12:56). It is not possible to do this in any detail in this document but we must start with at least the broad outlines of an analysis of the conflict in which we find ourselves.

It would be quite wrong to see the present conflict as simply a racial war. The racial component is there, but we are not dealing with two equal races or nations each with its own selfish group interests. The situation we are dealing with here is one of oppression. The conflict is between an oppressor and the oppressed. The conflict is between two irreconcilable *causes* or *interests* in which the one is just and the other is unjust.

On the one hand we have the interests of those who benefit from the status quo and who are determined to maintain it at any cost, even at the cost of millions of lives. It is in their interests to introduce a number of reforms in order to ensure that the system is not radically changed and that they can continue to benefit from it as they have done in the past. They benefit from the system because it favours them and enables them to accumulate a great deal of wealth and to maintain an exceptionally high standard of living. And they want to make sure that it stays that way even if some adjustments are needed.

On the other hand we have those who do not benefit in any way from the system the way it is now. They are treated as mere labour units, paid starvation wages, separated from their families by migratory labour, moved about like cattle and dumped in homelands to starve — and all for the benefit of a privileged minority. They have no say in the system and are supposed to be grateful for the concessions that are offered to them like crumbs. It is not in their interests to allow this system to continue even in some 'reformed' or 'revised' form. They are no longer prepared to be crushed, oppressed and exploited. They are determined to change the system radically so that it no longer benefits only the privileged few. And they are willing to do this even at the cost of their own lives. What they want is justice for all.

This is our situation of civil war or revolution. The one side is committed to maintaining the system at all costs and the other side is committed to changing it at all costs. There are two conflicting projects here and no compromise is possible. Either we have full and equal justice for all or we don't.

The Bible has a great deal to say about this kind of conflict, about a world that is divided into oppressors and oppressed.

4.2 Oppression in the Bible

When we search the Bible for a message about oppression we discover, as others throughout the world are discovering, that oppression is a central theme that runs right through the Old and New Testaments. The biblical scholars who have taken the trouble to study the theme of oppression in the Bible have discovered that there are no less than twenty different root words in Hebrew to describe oppression. As one author says, oppression is "a basic structural category of biblical theology" (T D Hanks, *God So Loved the Third World* [1983], p 4).

Moreover, the description of oppression in the Bible is concrete and vivid. The Bible describes oppression as the experience of being crushed, degraded, humiliated, exploited, impoverished, defrauded, deceived and enslaved. And the oppressors are described as cruel, ruthless, arrogant, greedy, violent and tyrannical and as the enemy. Such descriptions could only have been written originally by people who had had a long and painful experience of what it means to be oppressed. And indeed nearly 90 percent of the history of the Jewish and later the Christian people whose story is told in the Bible is a history of domestic or international oppression. Israel as a nation was built upon the painful experience of oppression and repression as slaves in Egypt. But what made all the difference for this particular group of oppressed people was the revelation of Yahweh. God revealed himself as Yahweh, the one who has compassion on those who suffer and who liberates them from their oppressors.

> I have seen the miserable state of my people in Egypt. I have heard their appeal to be free of their slave-drivers. I mean to deliver them out of the hands of the Egyptians. . . . The cry of the sons of Israel has come to me, and I have witnessed the way in which the Egyptians oppress them (Ex 3:7-9).

Throughout the Bible God appears as the liberator of the oppressed. He is not neutral. He does not attempt to reconcile Moses and Pharaoh, to reconcile the Hebrew slaves with their Egyptian oppressors or to reconcile the Jewish people with any of their later oppressors. Oppression is sin and it cannot be compromised with, it must be done away with. God takes sides with the oppressed. As we read in Psalm 103:6 (JB), "God, who does what is right, is always on the side of the oppressed."

Nor is this identification with the oppressed confined to the Old Testament. When Jesus stood up in the synagogue at Nazareth to announce his mission he made use of the words of Isaiah.

> The Spirit of the Lord has been given to me, for he has anointed me. He has sent me to bring the good news to the poor, to proclaim liberty to captives and to the blind new sight, to set the downtrodden free, to proclaim the Lord's year of favour (Lk 4:18-19).

There can be no doubt that Jesus is here taking up the cause of the poor and the oppressed. He has identified himself with their interests. Not that he is unconcerned about the rich and the oppressor. These he calls to repentance. The oppressed Christians of South Africa have known for a long time that they are united to Christ in their sufferings. By his own suffering and his death on the cross he became a victim of oppression and violence. He is with us in our oppression.

4.3 Tyranny in the Christian Tradition

There is a long Christian tradition relating to oppression, but the word that has been used most frequently to describe this particular form of sinfulness is the word 'tyranny'. According to this tradition once it is established beyond doubt that a particular ruler is a tyrant or that a particular regime is tyrannical, it forfeits the moral right to govern and the people acquire the right to resist and to find the means to protect their own interests against injustice and oppression. In other words a tyrannical regime has no *moral legitimacy*. It may be the *de facto* government and it may even be recognised by other governments and therefore be the *de iure* or legal government. But if it is a tyrannical regime, it is, from a moral and a theological point of view, *illegitimate*.

There are indeed some differences of opinion in the Christian tradition about the means that might be used to replace a tyrant *but* there has not been any doubt about our Christian duty to refuse to co-operate with tyranny and to do whatever we can to remove it.

Of course everything hinges on the definition of a tyrant. At what point does a government become a tyrannical regime?

The traditional Latin definition of a tyrant is *hostis boni communis* — an enemy of the common good. The purpose of all government is the promotion of what is called the common good of the people governed. To promote the common good is to govern in the interest of, and for the benefit of, all the people. Many governments fail to do this at times. There might be this or that injustice done to some of the people. And such lapses would indeed have to be criticised. But occasional acts of injustice would not make a government into an enemy of the people, a tyrant.

To be an enemy of the people a government would have to be hostile to the common good *in principle*.

Such a government would be acting against the interests of the people as a whole and permanently. This would be clearest in cases where the very policy of a government is hostile towards the common good and where the government has a mandate to rule in the interests of some of the people rather than in the interests of all the people. Such a government would be in principle *irreformable*. Any reform that it might try to introduce would not be calculated to serve the common good but to serve the interests of the minority from whom it received its mandate.

A tyrannical regime cannot continue to rule for very long without becoming more and more *violent*. As the majority of the people begin to demand their rights and to put pressure on the tyrant, so will the tyrant resort more and more to desperate, cruel, gross and ruthless forms of tyranny and repression. The reign of a tyrant always ends up as a reign of terror. It is inevitable because from the start the tyrant is an enemy of the common good.

This account of what we mean by a tyrant or a tyrannical regime can best be summed up in the words of a well-known moral theologian: "a regime which is openly the enemy of the people and which violates the common good permanently and in the grossest manner" (B Häring, *The Law of Christ*, Vol 3, p 150).

That leaves us with the question of whether the present government of South Africa is tyrannical or not. There can be no doubt what the majority of the people of South Africa think. For them the apartheid regime is indeed the enemy of the people and that is precisely what they call it: the enemy. In the present crisis, more than ever before, the regime has lost any legitimacy that it might have had in the eyes of the people. Are the people right or wrong?

Apartheid is a system whereby a minority regime elected by one small section of the population is given an explicit mandate to govern in the interests of, and for the benefit of, the white community. Such a mandate or policy is by definition hostile to the common good of all the people. In fact because it tries to rule in the exclusive interests of whites and not in the interests of all, it ends up ruling in a way that is not even in the interests of those same whites. It becomes an enemy of all the people. A tyrant. A totalitarian regime. A reign of terror.

This also means that the apartheid minority regime is irreformable. We cannot expect the apartheid regime to experience a conversion or change of heart and totally abandon the policy of apartheid. It has no mandate from its electorate to do so. Any reforms or adjustments it might make would have to be done in the interests of those who elected it. Individual members of the government could experience a real conversion and repent but, if they did, they would simply have to follow this through by leaving a regime that was elected and put into power precisely because of its policy of apartheid.

And that is why we have reached the present impasse. As the oppressed majority becomes more insistent and puts more and more pressure on the tyrant by means of boycotts, strikes, uprisings, burnings and even armed struggle, the more tyrannical will this regime become. On the one hand it will use repressive measures: detentions, trials, killings, torture, bannings, propaganda, states of emergency and other desperate and tyrannical methods. And on the other hand it will introduce reforms that will always be unacceptable to the majority because all its reforms must ensure that the white minority remains on top.

A regime that is in principle the enemy of the people cannot suddenly begin to rule in the interests of all the people. It can only be replaced by another government — one that has been elected by the majority of the people with an explicit mandate to govern in the interests of all the people.

A regime that has made itself the enemy of the people has thereby also made itself the enemy of God. People are made in the image and likeness of God and whatever we do to the least of them we do to God (Mt 25:40, 45).

To say that the State or the regime is the enemy of God is not to say that all those who support the system are aware of this. On the whole they simply do not know what they are doing. Many people have been blinded by the regime's propaganda. They are frequently quite ignorant of the consequences of their stance. However, such blindness does not make the State any less tyrannical or any less of an enemy of the people and an enemy of God.

On the other hand the fact that the State is tyrannical and an enemy of God is no excuse for hatred. As Christians we are called upon to love our enemies (Mt 5:44). It is not said that we should not or will not have enemies or that we should not identify tyrannical regimes as indeed our enemies. But once we have identified our enemies, we must endeavour to love them. That is not always easy. But then we must also remember that the most loving thing we can do for *both* the oppressed *and* for our enemies who are oppressors is to eliminate the oppression, remove the tyrants from power and establish a just government for the common good of *all the people.*

4.4 A Message of Hope

At the very heart of the gospel of Jesus Christ and at the very centre of all true prophecy is a message of hope. Nothing could be more relevant and more necessary at this moment of crisis in South Africa than the Christian message of hope.

Jesus has taught us to speak of this hope as the coming of God's kingdom. We believe that God is at work in our world turning hopeless and evil situations to good so that his "Kingdom may come" and his "Will may be done on earth as it is in heaven". We believe that goodness and justice and love will triumph in the end and that tyranny and oppression cannot last forever. One day "all tears will be wiped away" (Rev 7:17; 21:4) and "the lamb will lie down with the lion" (Is 11:6). True peace and true reconciliation are not only desirable, they are assured and guaranteed. This is our faith and our hope.

Why is it that this powerful message of hope has not been highlighted in 'Church Theology', in the statements and pronouncements of Church leaders? Is it because they have been addressing themselves to the oppressor rather than to the oppressed? Is it because they do not want to encourage the oppressed to be too hopeful for too much?

As the crisis deepens day by day, what both the oppressor and the oppressed can legitimately demand of the Churches is a message of hope. Most of the oppressed people in South Africa today and especially the youth do have hope. They are acting courageously and fearlessly because they have a sure hope that liberation will come. Often enough their bodies are broken but nothing can now break their spirit. But hope needs to be confirmed. Hope needs to be maintained and strengthened. Hope needs to be spread. The people need to hear it said again and again that God is with them.

On the other hand the oppressor and those who believe the propaganda of the oppressor are desperately fearful. They must be made aware of the diabolical evils of the present system and they must be called to repentance but they must also be given something to hope for. At present they have false hopes. They hope to maintain the status quo and their special privileges with perhaps some adjustments and they fear any real alternative. But there is much more than that to hope for and nothing to fear. Can the Christian message of hope not help them in this matter?

There is hope. There is hope for all of us. But the road to that hope is going to be very hard and very painful. The conflict and the struggle will have to intensify in the months and years ahead because there is no other way to remove the injustice and oppression. But God is with us. We can only learn to become the instruments of *his* peace even unto death. We must participate in the cross of Christ if we are to have the hope of participating in his resurrection.

Chapter Five

CHALLENGE TO ACTION

5.1 God Sides with the Oppressed

To say that the Church must now take sides unequivocally and consistently with the poor and the oppressed is to overlook the fact that the majority of Christians in South Africa have already done so. By far the greater part of the Church in South Africa *is* poor and oppressed. Of course it cannot be taken for granted that everyone who is oppressed has taken up their own cause and is struggling for their own liberation. Nor can it be assumed that all oppressed Christians are fully aware of the fact that their cause is God's cause. Nevertheless it remains true that the Church is already on the side of the oppressed because that is where the majority of its members are to be found. This fact needs to be appropriated and confirmed by the Church as a whole.

At the beginning of this document it was pointed out that the present crisis has highlighted the divisions in the Church. We are a divided Church precisely because not all the members of our Churches have taken sides against oppression. In other words not all Christians have united themselves with God "who is always on the side of the oppressed" (Ps 103:6). As far as the present crisis is concerned, there is only one way forward to Church unity, and that is for those Christians who find themselves on the side of the oppressor or sitting on the fence to cross over to the other side to be united in faith and action with those who are oppressed. Unity and reconciliation within the Church itself is only possible around God and Jesus Christ who are to be found on the side of the poor and the oppressed.

If this is what the Church must become, if this is what the Church as a whole must have as its project,

how then are we to translate it into concrete and effective action?

5.2 Participation in the Struggle
Christians, if they are not doing so already, must quite
simply participate in the struggle for liberation and for
a just society. The campaigns of the people, from con-
sumer boycotts to stayaways, need to be supported and
encouraged by the Church. Criticism will sometimes
be necessary but encouragement and support will also
be necessary. In other words the present crisis challenges the whole Church to move beyond a mere 'am-
bulance ministry' to a ministry of involvement and
participation.

5.3 Transforming Church Activities
The Church has its own specific activities: Sunday
services, communion services, baptisms, Sunday
school, funerals and so forth. It also has its specific
way of expressing its faith and its commitment, i.e. in
the form of confessions of faith. All of these activities
must be re-shaped to be more fully consistent with a
prophetic faith related to the KAIROS that God is of-
fering us today. The evil forces we speak of in baptism
must be named. We know what these evil forces are
in South Africa today. The unity and sharing we profess in our communion services or Masses must be
named. It is the solidarity of the people inviting all to
join in the struggle for God's peace in South Africa.
The repentance we preach must be named. It is repentance for our share of the guilt for the suffering and
oppression in our country.

Much of what we do in our Church services has lost its relevance to the poor and the oppressed. Our services and sacraments have been appropriated to serve the need of the individual for comfort and security. Now these same Church activities must be reappropriated to serve the real religious needs of all the people and to further the liberating mission of God and the Church in the world.

5.4 Special Campaigns

Over and above its regular activities the Church would need to have special programmes, projects and campaigns because of the special needs of the struggle for liberation in South Africa today. But there is a very important caution here. The Church must avoid becoming a 'Third Force', a force between the oppressor and the oppressed. The Church's programmes and campaigns must not duplicate what the people's organisations are already doing and, even more seriously, the Church must not confuse the issue by having programmes that run counter to the struggles of those political organisations that truly represent the grievances and demands of the people. Consultation, co-ordination and co-operation will be needed. We all have the same goals even when we differ about the final significance of what we are struggling for.

5.5 Civil Disobedience

Once it is established that the present regime has no moral legitimacy and is in fact a tyrannical regime certain things follow for the Church and its activities. In the first place *the Church cannot collaborate with tyranny.*

It cannot or should not do anything that appears to give legitimacy to a morally illegitimate regime. Secondly, the Church should not only pray for a change of government, it should also mobilise its members in every parish to begin to think and work and plan for a change of government in South Africa. We must begin to look ahead and begin working now with firm hope and faith for a better future. And finally the moral illegitimacy of the apartheid regime means that the Church will have to be involved at times in *civil disobedience*. A Church that takes its responsibilities seriously in these circumstances will sometimes have to confront and to disobey the State in order to obey God.

5.6 Moral Guidance

The people look to the Church, especially in the midst of our present crisis, for moral guidance. In order to provide this the Church must first make its stand absolutely clear and never tire of explaining and dialoguing about it. It must then help people to understand their rights and their duties. There must be no misunderstanding about the *moral duty* of all who are oppressed to resist oppression and to struggle for liberation and justice. The Church will also find that at times it does need to curb excesses and to appeal to the consciences of those who act thoughtlessly and wildly.

But the Church of Jesus Christ is not called to be a bastion of caution and moderation. The Church should challenge, inspire and motivate people. It has a message of the cross that inspires us to make sacrifices for justice and liberation. It has a message of hope that challenges us to wake up and to act with hope and confidence. The Church must preach this message not only in words and sermons and statements but also through its actions, programmes, campaigns and divine services.

CONCLUSION

As we said in the beginning, there is nothing final about this document. Our hope is that it will stimulate discussion, debate, reflection and prayer, but, above all, that it will lead to action. We invite all committed Christians to take this matter further, to do more research, to develop the themes we have presented here or to criticise them and to return to the Bible, as we have tried to do, with the question raised by the crisis of our times.

Although the document suggests various modes of involvement it does not prescribe the particular actions anyone should take. We call upon all those who are committed to this prophetic form of theology to use the document for discussion in groups, small and big, to determine an appropriate form of action, depending on their particular situation, and to take up the action with other related groups and organisations.

The challenge to renewal and action that we have set out here is addressed to the Church. But that does not mean that it is intended only for Church leaders. The challenge of the faith and of our present KAIROS is addressed to all who bear the name Christian. None of us can simply sit back and wait to be told what to do by our Church leaders or by anyone else. We must all accept responsibility for acting and living out our Christian faith in these circumstances. We pray that God will help all of us to translate the challenge of our times into action.

We, as theologians (both lay and professional), have been greatly challenged by our own reflections, our exchange of ideas and our discoveries as we met together in smaller and larger groups to prepare this document or to suggest amendments to it. We are convinced that this challenge comes from God and that it is addressed to all of us. We see the present crisis or KAIROS as indeed a divine visitation.

And finally we also like to call upon our Christian brothers and sisters throughout the world to give us the necessary support in this regard so that the daily loss of so many young lives may be brought to a speedy end.

SIGNATORIES

We, the undersigned, take joint responsibility for what is presented in this document, not as a final statement of the truth but as the direction in which God is leading us at this moment of our history.

Name	Church
Dr. J.C. Adonis	Belydendekring
L.A. Appies	Dutch Reformed Mission Church
Ms. Mary Armour	Roman Catholic
Dr. J-F. Bill	Evangelical Presbyterian
Rev. N. Bixa	Methodist
Rev. A. Bhiman	Dutch Reformed Mission Church
Rev. N. Botha	Dutch Reformed Mission Church
Rev. A. Boer	Dutch Reformed Mission Church
Rev. A. Booyse	A.M.E.
Rev. A.S. Brews	Methodist
Ms. S. Britton	Anglican
Rev. J. Carnow	A.M.E.
Sis. F. Cassidy	Roman Catholic
Mr. Tony Chetty	Roman Catholic
Rev. F. Chikane	Apostolic Faith Mission
Dr. J. Cochrane	United Congregational
Rev. R. Cochrane	Lutheran
Dr. G.D. Cloete	Dutch Reformed Mission Church
Mr. W. Cloete	Sending Kerk
Mr. Roy Crowder	Methodist
Canon C. Davids	Anglican
Mr. Mike Deeb	Roman Catholic
Mr. S. De Gruchy	United Congregational
Prof. J.W. De Gruchy	United Congregational
Rev. J. De Waal	Dutch Reformed Mission Church
Dr. W. Domeris	Anglican
Rev. J.H. Dyers	Anglican
Ms. J.W. Engelbrecht	Assemblies of God
Rev. B.B. Finca	Reformed Presbyterian
Mr. P.A. Germond	Anglican
Dr. B. Goba	United Congregational

Fr. G. Gobaiyer	Roman Catholic
Rev. D.N. Goga	Reformed Presbyterian
Rev. S. Govender	Dutch Reformed Mission Church
Dr. T.S.N. Gqubule	Methodist
Mr. Paul Graham	Methodist
Rev. G. Grosser	German Lutheran
Rev. B. Habelgaarn	Moravian
Sis. Aine Hardiman	Roman Catholic
Sis. Clare Harkin	Roman Catholic
Rev. A. Hendricks	Methodist
Fr: Basil Hendricks	Roman Catholic
Rev. B. Hoorn	A.M.E.
Rev. R. Jacobus	Dutch Reformed Mission Church
Dr. Lizo Jafta	Methodist
Ms. Jaye Joubert	Methodist
Rev. Frans Kekana	International Assemblies of God
Fr. X. Keteyi	Roman Catholic
Mr. K. Kiefer	German Lutheran
Dr. W. Kistner	Lutheran
Rev. H.M. Koaho	Belydendekring
Rev. C.T. Kokoali	Anglican
Rev. J.N.J. Kritzinger	Belydendekring
Rev. C. Langeveld	Roman Catholic
Rev. Charl le Roux	N.G. Kerk
Rev. C.W. Leeuw	Reformed Presbyterian
Rev. T. Lester	Anglican
Rev. P.T. Letlala	Anglican
Mr. J. Liddell	Methodist
Ms. L. Liddell	Methodist
Rev. A.M. Lindhorst	Anglican
Mr. D. Loff	United Congregational
Rev. Gerrie Lubbe	Reformed Church of S.A.
Mrs. M. Mabaso	Lutheran
Rev. Lucas Mabusela	N.G. Kerk
Mr. Wesley Mabuza	Methodist
Venerable Archdeacon E. Mackenzie	Anglican
Prof. S.S. Maimela	Evangelical Lutheran
Rev. J.F. Mahlaseala	Methodist
Rev. C.J. Martin	United Congregational
Rev. Maake Masango	Presbyterian

Rev. S. Masemola	Anglican
Mrs. S. Mazibuko	Roman Catholic
Rev. O. Mbangula	Methodist
Rev. G.T. Mcoteli	Reformed Presbyterian
Rev. P.N. Mentoor	A.M.E.
Dr. K.E. Mgojo	Methodist
Fr. S. Mkhatshwa	Roman Catholic
Rev. M. Mnguni	Lutheran
Rev. Z. Mokhoebo	N.G. Kerk
Rev. Kenosi Mofokeng	National Baptist
Rev. S. Mogoba	Methodist
Mr. C. Molebatsi	Ebenezer Evangelical Church
Mr. Peter Moll	United Congregational
Fr. M.S.L. Monjane	Anglican
Mrs. B. Mosala	Roman Catholic
Dr. M. Motlhabi	Roman Catholic
Rev. M. Mpumlwana	Order of Ethiopian Church
Vicar F. Müller	Lutheran
Mrs. M. Mxadana	Anglican
Mrs. L. Myeza	Methodist
Dr. B. Naude	N.G. Kerk
Dr. Margaret Nash	Anglican
Sis. B. Ncube	Roman Catholic
Pastor Z. Nertuch	Lutheran
Rev. H. Ngada	United Independent Believer in Christ
Rev. S.B. Ngcobo	Reformed Presbyterian
Rev. D. Nkwe	Anglican
Dr. A. Nolan	Roman Catholic
Rev. P.A. Nordengen	Lutheran
Fr. S. Ntwasa	Anglican
Rev. T.W. Ntongana	Apostolic Methodist Church of S.A.
Mr. R. Nunes	Roman Catholic
Rev. R.T. Nyanela	Reformed Presbyterian
Rev. M. Nyawo	Evangelical Presbyterian
Fr. R. O'Rouke	Roman Catholic
Rev. C. Onthong	Anglican
Rev. T. Pearce	Anglican
Rev. G.B. Peter	Reformed Church in Africa
Ms. Debora Petta	United Congregational
Mr. R.E. Phillips	Anglican
Rev. Robin Peterson	United Congregational
Mr. V.P. Peterson	Anglican
Ms. Heather Peterson	United Congregational

Canon G. Quinlan	Anglican
Mrs. A. Rathebe	Anglican
Rev. W. Saayman	N.G. Kerk
Rev. C. Sampson	Anglican
Fr. L. Sebidi	Roman Catholic
Prof. G. Setiloane	Roman Catholic
Rev. J.N. Silwanyana	Methodist
Rev. A.L. Smith	Anglican
Rev. Nico Smith	N.G. Kerk in Afrika
Rev. E.T. Soeldner	Lutheran
Rev. Z. Somana	Methodist
Rev. M.A. Stofile	Presbyterian
Fr. F. Synnott	Roman Catholic
Fr. Thami Tana	Roman Catholic
Rev. E. Tema	N.G. Kerk in Afrika
Mr. S. Thaver	Reformed Church in Africa
Mr. B. Theron	United Congregational
Rev. M. Tisani	Anglican
Rev. S. Titus	United Congregational
Fr. B. Tlhagale	Roman Catholic
Rev. M. Tsele	Lutheran
Rev. J. Tshawane	Evangelical Presbyterian
Rev. B. Tshipa	Lutheran
Rev. Van Den Heever	Sending Kerk
Mr. K. Vermeulen	Methodist
Dr. C. Villa-Vincencio	Methodist
Rev. A. Visagie	Dutch Reformed Mission Church
Rev. H. Visser	Sending Kerk
Rev. M.R. Vithi	Methodist
Dr. C.A. Wanamaker	United Congregational
Rev. Stephen Warnes	Anglican
Rev. M.I. Weeder	Anglican
Rev. D. White	Anglican
Ms. J. Williams	Anglican
Rev. B. Witbooi	Anglican
Fr. A. Winston	Roman Catholic
Mr. R.G. Wortley	Anglican

We realise that many others would probably have wanted to add their names to this list. Unfortunately, for a variety of reasons including time, distance and availability, we were not able to reach everyone who might have been interested.